Build Your Own Video Streaming Empire

The Ultimate Guide to Creating a Profitable Platform from Scratch

By

STEM School

This Page Left Intentionally Blank

Contents

Chapter 1

Introduction to Video Streaming

Video streaming is the process of delivering digital video content over the internet in real-time or on-demand without requiring users to download the entire file before playback. This technology allows viewers to watch videos instantly while data packets are continuously sent from the server to the user's device.

At its core, video streaming relies on data compression and transmission over networks. A video file is first encoded using compression techniques to reduce file size while maintaining quality. The encoded data is then transmitted through a Content Delivery Network (CDN) or a server, broken into smaller packets, and sent over internet protocols. These packets are reassembled by the user's media player to provide seamless playback. The entire process is supported by buffering mechanisms to prevent interruptions due to network fluctuations.

Streaming is typically classified into two categories live streaming and on-demand streaming. Live streaming occurs in real-time, such as broadcasting a sports event or a live webinar. In contrast, on-demand streaming allows users to access pre-recorded content, such as movies or television series, anytime they choose.

The efficiency of video streaming depends on several technical factors, including bandwidth availability, compression standards, and network latency. The better these parameters are optimized, the smoother the user experience.

The History of Streaming Technologies

The origins of video streaming can be traced back to the early days of the internet when bandwidth limitations made digital media delivery a challenge. Before streaming, users had to download entire video files, which took significant time and storage space. The development of streaming protocols changed this, allowing users to play content while it was still being downloaded in segments.

In the 1990s, companies like RealNetworks pioneered the first streaming media services, introducing RealAudio and RealVideo. These early efforts were hindered by slow internet speeds and limited computing power. However, as broadband technology advanced, streaming became more viable.

By the early 2000s, Adobe Flash Player revolutionized video streaming by enabling smooth playback in web browsers. This period saw the rise of YouTube in 2005, marking a turning point in online video consumption. As mobile devices and internet speeds improved, streaming services expanded, leading to the rise of Netflix, Hulu, and Amazon Prime Video.

In recent years, newer technologies such as Adaptive Bitrate Streaming (ABR), HTTP Live Streaming (HLS), and MPEG-DASH have further improved the streaming experience. These technologies allow videos to adjust quality dynamically based on the user's network conditions, ensuring uninterrupted viewing. Additionally, cloud-based solutions and AI-driven optimizations have made video streaming more efficient and accessible worldwide.

The table below summarizes the key milestones in the evolution of video streaming

Year	Milestone Description
1995	RealNetworks introduces RealAudio, an early form of streaming media.
1997	Microsoft launches Windows Media Player with streaming support.
2000	Adobe Flash becomes the dominant streaming format for web-based video.
2005	YouTube is founded, bringing user-generated video content into the mainstream.

Year	Milestone Description
2007	Netflix launches its streaming service, revolutionizing digital media consumption.
2010	Apple introduces HTTP Live Streaming (HLS), improving video delivery on mobile devices.
2015	Facebook Live and Periscope popularize real-time live streaming.
2020	AI-driven video compression and cloud streaming services gain traction.

On-Demand vs. Live Streaming

Video streaming falls into two major categories on-demand and live streaming. Each serves different purposes and comes with its own advantages and challenges.

On-demand streaming refers to pre-recorded content that users can access anytime, similar to watching a movie on Netflix or a tutorial on YouTube. This type of streaming allows for extensive content libraries, flexible viewing schedules, and optimized video quality through buffering and preloading.

On the other hand, live streaming delivers real-time content, making it ideal for events such as sports broadcasts, concerts, and webinars. Since it occurs in real-time, it is highly engaging and fosters direct audience interaction. However, live streaming is more challenging due to latency issues, bandwidth fluctuations, and the inability to edit content before broadcasting.

The table below compares these two types of streaming

Feature	On-Demand Streaming	Live Streaming
Content Type	Pre-recorded videos (movies, TV shows, courses)	Real-time broadcasts (sports, concerts, live news)
Playback Control	Users can pause, rewind, or fast-forward	Viewers must watch in real-time
Quality Optimization	High-quality with buffering and adaptive bitrate	Dependent on network stability
Interaction	Limited or pre-set engagement (comments, likes)	High engagement through live chats, reactions
Technical Complexity	Easier to manage and distribute	Requires low latency and real-time

Feature	On-Demand Streaming	Live Streaming
		encoding

Key Components of Video Streaming

Several critical components ensure smooth and efficient video streaming

Encoding and Compression Raw video files are too large for direct streaming, so they must be compressed using codecs like H.264, H.265 (HEVC), or VP9. These codecs reduce file size while maintaining visual quality. Encoding transforms video files into streamable formats, making playback possible on various devices.

Content Delivery Network (CDN) A CDN is a network of distributed servers that store and deliver video content efficiently. CDNs help reduce buffering, improve loading speeds, and prevent server overloads by caching content at multiple locations worldwide. Popular CDNs include Akamai, Cloudflare, and Amazon CloudFront.

Streaming Protocols Protocols dictate how video data is transmitted over the internet. The most widely used streaming protocols include

- **HLS (HTTP Live Streaming)** Developed by Apple, this protocol delivers adaptive bitrate streaming and is compatible with most devices.
- **DASH (Dynamic Adaptive Streaming over HTTP)** A widely used alternative to HLS, offering similar functionality but not restricted to Apple devices.
- **RTMP (Real-Time Messaging Protocol)** Originally used for Flash streaming, now mostly used for live streaming to platforms like YouTube and Facebook Live.

Storage and Hosting Videos must be stored in a way that allows quick retrieval and seamless playback. Cloud-based storage solutions such as AWS S3, Google Cloud, and Azure Media Services offer scalable and cost-efficient video hosting options.

The following diagram illustrates the video streaming workflow

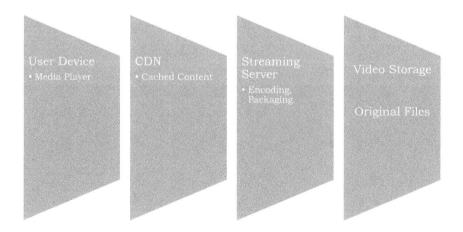

User Device
• Media Player

CDN
• Cached Content

Streaming Server
• Encoding, Packaging

Video Storage

Original Files

This simplified model shows how video content moves from storage to the end user, passing through CDNs and encoding processes to ensure smooth playback.

Video streaming has revolutionized content consumption, allowing instant access to media on various devices. Understanding its history, key components, and technological advancements helps businesses and individuals leverage this powerful medium effectively. As internet speeds continue to improve and AI-driven optimizations improve content delivery, streaming will continue evolving, shaping the future of digital entertainment and communication.

Chapter 2

Planning and Architecture

Building a video streaming platform begins with clearly defining its scope and features. A successful platform must align with the needs of its target audience, technical capabilities, and business goals. Before delving into the technical implementation, it is essential to establish a clear vision for what the platform will offer.

The scope of a video streaming platform depends on whether it will focus on live streaming, on-demand content, or both. For example, a platform like Netflix primarily offers on-demand streaming, whereas Twitch and YouTube Live specialize in live content delivery. The type of content also determines the necessary infrastructure, storage, and network requirements.

Key features of a streaming platform include content upload and management, encoding and compression, content distribution via a CDN, user authentication, monetization options, analytics, and security. These features impact the architecture and require careful planning to ensure smooth operation.

A basic framework for defining the scope can be outlined in the table below

Feature Category	Description	Examples of Implementation
Content	Determines how	On-demand, live

Feature Category	Description	Examples of Implementation
Delivery	content is streamed to users	streaming, hybrid
User Access Control	Defines how users access content	Free, subscription-based, pay-per-view
Monetization	Revenue generation options	Advertisements, subscriptions, sponsorships
Security	Protection against piracy and unauthorized access	DRM, watermarking, encryption
Analytics	Provides insights into user behavior and performance	Viewer engagement, watch time, server load
Device Compatibility	Ensures seamless playback across multiple devices	Web, mobile, smart TV, gaming consoles

Each of these factors must be carefully considered to align with the platform's goals, ensuring that the right technologies are selected to support them.

Cloud-Based or Self-Hosted Solutions

When building a streaming platform, one of the most critical decisions is whether to use a cloud-based or self-hosted solution. Each approach has distinct advantages and challenges, and the choice depends on factors such as budget, scalability requirements, technical expertise, and security concerns.

A cloud-based solution leverages third-party cloud services such as AWS, Google Cloud, or Microsoft Azure to handle video storage, processing, and distribution. This option offers scalability, reliability, and reduced maintenance overhead since the cloud provider manages hardware, software updates, and security. Cloud services often come with built-in content delivery networks (CDNs), which optimize performance for global audiences.

In contrast, a self-hosted solution involves deploying video streaming infrastructure on privately managed servers. This approach provides greater control over data security and system configurations. However, it requires extensive technical expertise to manage server maintenance, scaling, and security protocols.

The following table compares cloud-based and self-hosted solutions

Criteria	Cloud-Based Solution	Self-Hosted Solution

Criteria	Cloud-Based Solution	Self-Hosted Solution
Cost	Pay-as-you-go model, costs scale with usage	Higher initial investment, but lower long-term costs
Scalability	Highly scalable, auto-scaling capabilities	Requires manual infrastructure scaling
Security	Managed security protocols and encryption	Full control over data security measures
Maintenance	Minimal maintenance; handled by the provider	Requires dedicated IT resources
Performance	Optimized with global CDNs	Performance depends on server configuration
Customization	Limited to available services	Full customization options

Cloud-based solutions are ideal for businesses that need quick deployment and scalability without extensive infrastructure management. Self-hosting, on the other hand, is suitable for organizations that require complete control over data and security, particularly in industries with strict regulatory compliance.

High-Level Architecture of a Video Streaming

The architecture of a video streaming platform consists of multiple components that work together to encode, store, deliver, and play video content efficiently. A high-level streaming architecture typically includes

Content Ingestion and Encoding – The raw video content is ingested into the system, where it undergoes encoding and compression using codecs such as H.264, H.265, or VP9. Encoding is necessary to reduce file size while maintaining video quality.

Content Storage – The encoded videos are stored in either cloud-based storage (AWS S3, Google Cloud Storage) or private servers. Storage solutions must support fast retrieval and redundancy to prevent data loss.

Content Distribution (CDN) – A Content Delivery Network (CDN) helps distribute video content efficiently by caching it in multiple locations worldwide, reducing latency and buffering issues.

Streaming Protocols – Various protocols manage video delivery. HTTP Live Streaming (HLS) and MPEG-

DASH are widely used adaptive bitrate streaming technologies that adjust quality based on network conditions.

User Authentication & Access Control – Secure authentication methods, such as OAuth, token-based access, and DRM (Digital Rights Management), ensure that content is protected against unauthorized use.

Playback & User Experience – The final component involves the video player and front-end interface, which must be optimized for multiple devices, including desktops, mobile devices, and smart TVs.

This modular approach allows flexibility and scalability, ensuring that each component can be optimized independently.

Scalability and Performance Considerations

Scalability is one of the most crucial factors in building a streaming platform, as user demand can vary significantly based on peak usage times and geographic location. The ability to handle a sudden surge in viewers without degradation in quality is key to providing a seamless experience.

Performance is affected by factors such as network bandwidth, server load, and latency. A well-designed streaming architecture must incorporate solutions to optimize speed, reliability, and efficiency.

To achieve scalability, platforms typically implement

Load Balancing Distributing traffic across multiple servers to prevent bottlenecks and reduce the risk of failures. Load balancers dynamically allocate resources based on demand.

Auto-Scaling Infrastructure Cloud-based platforms use auto-scaling mechanisms that add or remove instances based on traffic. This ensures that resources are efficiently allocated, reducing costs during low traffic periods.

Edge Computing with CDNs Placing content closer to users via a CDN reduces latency and improves playback performance.

Optimized Encoding & Adaptive Bitrate Streaming Encoding content at multiple resolutions and bitrates allows the streaming player to adjust quality in real-time based on the viewer's internet speed.

The table below outlines key scalability strategies

Strategy	Benefit	Example Implementation
Load Balancing	Distributes traffic to prevent overload	Nginx, AWS Elastic Load Balancer

Strategy	Benefit	Example Implementation
Auto-Scaling	Automatically adjusts resources	Kubernetes, AWS Auto Scaling
CDN Integration	Reduces latency and improves speed	Cloudflare, Akamai, Fastly
Multi-Bitrate Streaming	Ensures smooth playback under varying network conditions	HLS, DASH

Efficient monitoring tools such as Prometheus, Grafana, and AWS CloudWatch can also provide real-time insights into server performance, helping to detect issues before they impact users.

Planning the architecture of a video streaming platform requires careful consideration of its scope, hosting options, system design, and scalability. A cloud-based approach offers flexibility and ease of management, while a self-hosted solution provides greater control and customization. The high-level architecture must be designed to ensure smooth content delivery, with key components working seamlessly together. Scalability and performance considerations play a vital role in providing an uninterrupted streaming experience, making it essential to implement strategies like load balancing, CDNs, and adaptive bitrate streaming.

By understanding these foundational concepts, developers and businesses can build a robust, future-proof video streaming platform that meets the demands of a growing digital audience.

Chapter 3

Understanding Video Formats and Codecs

Video formats play a crucial role in determining how multimedia files are stored, transmitted, and played on different devices. Each format consists of a container that holds video, audio, and metadata, making it essential to choose the right format based on compatibility, compression efficiency, and playback requirements.

One of the most widely used formats is **MP4 (MPEG-4 Part 14)**, known for its high compatibility with various devices, web platforms, and media players. It supports multiple codecs, including H.264 and H.265, making it a preferred choice for online streaming and mobile playback. Due to its balance between quality and file size, MP4 remains the industry standard for video distribution.

Another widely used format is **MKV (Matroska Video)**, which is an open-source container format that supports multiple audio and subtitle tracks within a single file. MKV is ideal for high-definition movies and digital archiving due to its flexibility and ability to store lossless video and audio. However, it is not as universally supported as MP4, which limits its use for web-based streaming.

For Apple ecosystem users, **MOV (QuickTime File Format)** is a popular choice. Originally developed by Apple, MOV is optimized for QuickTime Player and macOS applications. It offers high-quality video playback but often results in larger file sizes compared to MP4, making it less suitable for streaming.

One of the older but still relevant formats is **AVI (Audio Video Interleave),** developed by Microsoft. AVI is known for its minimal compression, resulting in large file sizes but high video quality. Despite its age, it remains in use for specific applications, especially in professional video editing environments. However, its lack of efficient compression makes it impractical for modern streaming platforms.

The table below summarizes the key characteristics of these video formats

Format	Developer	Compression Efficiency	Compatibility	Best Use Cases
MP4	MPEG	High	Universal (Web, Mobile, Streaming)	Online streaming, mobile playback
MKV	Matroska	Medium	Limited (Not supported by some devices)	HD movies, multiple audio/subtitle tracks
MOV	Apple	High	Apple	Video

Format	Developer	Compression Efficiency	Compatibility	Best Use Cases
			ecosystem	editing, macOS applications
AVI	Microsoft	Low	Windows & some players	Professional video editing, lossless video

Understanding Video and Audio Codecs

A video codec is a technology used to encode and compress video data to make it more efficient for storage and transmission. Without codecs, video files would be excessively large, making them difficult to stream over the internet. The two most important factors in a codec are compression efficiency and playback quality.

One of the most widely used video codecs is **H.264 (Advanced Video Coding, AVC)**, which balances compression efficiency and video quality. H.264 is supported by almost every media player, browser, and streaming service, making it the industry standard for online video.

A more advanced and efficient codec is **H.265 (High-Efficiency Video Coding, HEVC),** which provides up to 50% better compression than H.264 while maintaining the same quality. This makes it ideal for high-definition and 4K streaming, but it requires more processing power for encoding and decoding.

For open-source enthusiasts, **VP9**, developed by Google, is an alternative codec that delivers high compression efficiency similar to H.265 but is royalty-free. VP9 is widely used on YouTube and other web platforms, reducing bandwidth consumption while maintaining visual quality.

In addition to video codecs, audio codecs play a critical role in streaming. **AAC (Advanced Audio Codec)** is the most commonly used audio format, providing high-quality sound at lower bitrates. It is widely supported across mobile devices and streaming services.

Another efficient audio codec is **Opus**, which offers superior compression while maintaining audio fidelity. Opus is especially useful for real-time applications such as VoIP, live streaming, and conferencing.

The table below compares the major video and audio codecs

Codec	Type	Compression Efficiency	Best Use Cases	Support
H.264	Video	Medium	General video streaming, YouTube, mobile	Universal
H.265 (HEVC)	Video	High	4K streaming, Ultra HD video	Limited (requires powerful devices)
VP9	Video	High	Web streaming, YouTube, royalty-free usage	Supported in modern browsers
AAC	Audio	High	Music streaming, mobile devices	Universal
Opus	Audio	Very High	Live streaming, VoIP, conferencing	Supported in modern applications

Choosing the Right Codec for Efficiency

Selecting the right codec depends on multiple factors, including the target platform, bandwidth availability, and playback device capabilities.

For general web-based streaming, **H.264 remains the most practical choice** due to its broad support and balance between file size and quality. However, platforms requiring higher resolution, such as **4K or HDR streaming, benefit from H.265 (HEVC),** which provides better compression but demands more processing power.

When targeting web-based applications where royalty fees for H.265 are a concern, **VP9 is a great alternative**. It is widely supported on YouTube and modern web browsers, making it a viable choice for high-quality video streaming.

For live streaming applications, **low-latency encoding is crucial**. H.264 and VP9 perform well, but **Opus is the best choice for real-time audio due to its superior efficiency and adaptability.**

In cases where compatibility across all devices is a priority, H.264 and AAC provide the most reliable combination. The trade-off is that newer codecs like H.265 and VP9 offer better efficiency but require updated hardware for smooth playback.

The choice of codec significantly impacts bandwidth consumption. The table below illustrates the bitrate requirements for different codecs at various resolutions

Resolution	H.264 Bitrate	H.265 Bitrate	VP9 Bitrate
720p	2.5 Mbps	1.5 Mbps	1.6 Mbps
1080p	5 Mbps	3 Mbps	2.8 Mbps
4K UHD	25 Mbps	15 Mbps	14 Mbps

By selecting the appropriate codec, streaming platforms can optimize bandwidth usage while ensuring high-quality playback.

Transcoding and Adaptive Bitrate Streaming

Transcoding is a vital process in video streaming that involves converting a video from one format or resolution to another. This ensures that the video can be played on different devices and network conditions. The process typically includes re-encoding the video using different bitrates and resolutions.

Adaptive Bitrate Streaming (ABR) is a technique that dynamically adjusts the quality of a video stream based on the user's internet speed. Instead of delivering a single file, ABR creates multiple versions of the same video at different resolutions and bitrates. The streaming player then selects the best version based on real-time network conditions.

A typical ABR workflow follows these steps

1. The original video is uploaded and encoded into multiple formats and resolutions.
2. A streaming server stores these versions and delivers them via a CDN.
3. The user's media player continuously monitors bandwidth conditions and switches between different resolutions to maintain smooth playback.

The diagram below illustrates how ABR works

This technique ensures that users with fast internet connections receive high-quality streams, while those with slower networks can still watch without buffering interruptions.

Understanding video formats, codecs, and transcoding processes is essential for optimizing video streaming platforms. The right choice of format and codec can significantly impact video quality, storage, and bandwidth consumption. While MP4 with H.264 remains the most widely supported combination, newer codecs like H.265 and VP9 provide better efficiency for high-resolution content. Adaptive Bitrate Streaming further improves the viewing experience by dynamically adjusting quality based on network conditions. By mastering these elements, streaming platforms can deliver a seamless, high-quality experience to users across various devices and internet speeds.

Chapter 4

Setting Up a Media Server

A media server is a specialized software or hardware solution designed to store, process, and distribute audio and video content over a network. These servers play a critical role in modern video streaming by efficiently handling both live and on-demand content. A well-configured media server ensures seamless playback, supports multiple formats and protocols, and optimizes bandwidth usage to deliver high-quality streaming experiences.

There are several widely used media servers available today, each offering unique features tailored for different streaming needs.

Wowza Streaming Engine is a powerful, enterprise-grade media server that supports live and on-demand streaming across multiple devices. It offers advanced features such as real-time transcoding, adaptive bitrate streaming, and cloud integration. Wowza is widely used in professional broadcasting, education, and corporate environments.

Red5 Media Server is an open-source streaming server that supports live video broadcasting, video conferencing, and VoIP applications. It is built on Java and provides extensive support for RTMP (Real-Time Messaging Protocol) streaming. Red5 is commonly used in interactive applications such as webinars and gaming platforms.

Nginx RTMP Module is a lightweight and efficient solution for streaming video content over RTMP and HLS. It is an extension of the popular Nginx web server and provides high-performance media streaming with minimal resource consumption. Due to its scalability and low cost, Nginx RTMP is an excellent choice for startups and independent broadcasters.

Ant Media Server is a flexible and scalable media server that supports low-latency streaming using WebRTC, RTMP, and HLS. It is designed for applications requiring real-time video delivery, such as online gaming, telemedicine, and interactive live streaming. Ant Media Server also offers adaptive bitrate streaming and cloud-based deployment options.

The table below provides a comparison of these media servers

Media Server	Open Source	Supported Protocols	Best Use Cases	Scalability
Wowza Streaming Engine	No	RTMP, HLS, DASH, WebRTC	Enterprise streaming, professional broadcasting	High
Red5 Media	Yes	RTMP	Webinars, video	Medium

Media Server	Open Source	Supported Protocols	Best Use Cases	Scalability
Server			conferencing, gaming	
Nginx RTMP	Yes	RTMP, HLS	Independent streaming, startups	High
Ant Media Server	No	RTMP, HLS, WebRTC	Low-latency streaming, real-time applications	High

Installation of a Media Server

Setting up a media server involves installing the necessary software, configuring streaming settings, and optimizing performance to ensure smooth video delivery. The installation process varies depending on the chosen media server and hosting environment.

For example, installing **Nginx with RTMP module** on a Linux-based system follows these steps

Update the system and install dependencies

sudo apt update
sudo apt install build-essential libpcre3 libpcre3-dev zlib1g zlib1g-dev libssl-dev

Download and compile Nginx with RTMP module

```
wget http //nginx.org/download/nginx-1.21.3.tar.gz
wget          https          //github.com/arut/nginx-rtmp-
module/archive/master.zip
tar -zxvf nginx-1.21.3.tar.gz
unzip master.zip
cd nginx-1.21.3
./configure  --add-module=../nginx-rtmp-module-master  --with-
http_ssl_module
make
sudo make install
```

Configure RTMP streaming in the Nginx configuration file (/usr/local/nginx/conf/nginx.conf)

```
rtmp {
   server {
      listen 1935;
      application live {
         live on;
         record off;
      }
   }
}
```

1. **Restart Nginx and start streaming**

```
sudo /usr/local/nginx/sbin/nginx
```

For **Wowza Streaming Engine**, the installation process involves downloading the official software, setting up a license, and configuring streaming sources through the Wowza control panel.

Streaming Protocols RTMP, HLS, DASH

To deliver video content efficiently, media servers rely on different streaming protocols. Each protocol is designed to cater to specific use cases, ensuring seamless playback across a variety of devices and network conditions.

RTMP (Real-Time Messaging Protocol) is a low-latency protocol widely used for live video streaming. It enables fast transmission of video data between an encoder and a media server, making it suitable for live broadcasts. However, RTMP is gradually being replaced by newer protocols due to limited browser support.

HLS (HTTP Live Streaming) is an adaptive streaming protocol developed by Apple. It breaks video into small chunks and delivers them via HTTP, ensuring smooth playback even under fluctuating network conditions. HLS is widely supported on iOS, Android, and web browsers, making it a preferred choice for video-on-demand services.

DASH (Dynamic Adaptive Streaming over HTTP) is a similar protocol to HLS but is not tied to any specific platform. It provides adaptive bitrate streaming by dynamically adjusting video quality based on network bandwidth. DASH is widely used by platforms like YouTube and Netflix.

WebRTC (Web Real-Time Communication) is a low-latency protocol designed for real-time video streaming. Unlike other protocols, WebRTC allows peer-to-peer communication without requiring a dedicated media server. It is widely used in video conferencing, live auctions, and interactive applications.

The following diagram illustrates how these protocols function in a typical streaming setup

Handling Live and On-Demand Video

A media server must be capable of handling both live and on-demand streaming efficiently.

Live streaming involves capturing real-time video content and delivering it to viewers with minimal delay. To achieve this, the media server receives an RTMP stream from the broadcaster, processes it, and delivers it to users through HLS, DASH, or WebRTC. Low-latency streaming techniques, such as chunked transfer encoding and WebRTC, are often used to reduce delays.

On-demand video streaming refers to pre-recorded content stored on a server and delivered to users when requested. In this case, the media server retrieves the video file, transcodes it if necessary, and streams it using HLS or DASH. Adaptive bitrate streaming ensures smooth playback across different devices and network conditions.

The workflow for both live and on-demand streaming is shown in the diagram below

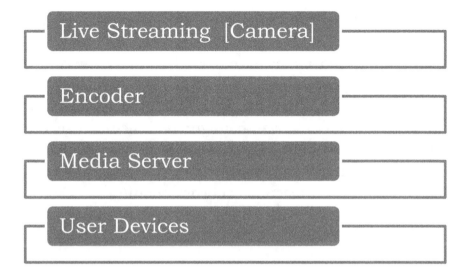

To improve performance, caching and Content Delivery Networks (CDNs) can be integrated into the media server architecture. A **CDN helps distribute video content across multiple servers worldwide**, reducing buffering and latency for end users.

Setting up a media server is a crucial step in building a reliable video streaming platform. Choosing the right media server depends on factors such as scalability, protocol support, and latency requirements. The installation process varies across different solutions, with options ranging from lightweight Nginx RTMP setups to feature-rich Wowza Streaming Engine deployments.

Understanding streaming protocols such as RTMP, HLS, DASH, and WebRTC is essential for delivering optimized video experiences. Each protocol serves a specific purpose, from low-latency live streaming to adaptive bitrate playback for on-demand content. By implementing a well-configured media server, streaming platforms can efficiently handle both live and on-demand video, ensuring high-quality playback across diverse devices and network conditions.

Chapter 5

Implementing a Content Delivery Network (CDN)

A **Content Delivery Network (CDN)** is an essential component of modern video streaming infrastructure, designed to improve the delivery speed, reliability, and scalability of video content across the internet. In simple terms, a CDN is a globally distributed network of servers that cache and serve video content from locations closest to the end user. This reduces latency, minimizes buffering, and ensures a smoother streaming experience.

The primary function of a CDN in video streaming is to **reduce the distance between the user and the content source**. Without a CDN, every request for a video stream would be routed to the origin server, causing congestion, increased load times, and possible service failures under high traffic conditions. A CDN alleviates this by replicating content across multiple geographically distributed edge servers, allowing users to access video files from the nearest node rather than the central server.

A CDN also **improves bandwidth efficiency** by offloading traffic from the origin server, ensuring that multiple users streaming the same content do not overwhelm a single server. This is particularly beneficial for large-scale video streaming platforms, where millions of users may be accessing content simultaneously.

Setting Up Own CDN vs. Third-Party Services

Organizations looking to implement a CDN for video streaming face a crucial decision **should they build their own CDN or leverage third-party services such as Cloudflare, AWS CloudFront, or Akamai?** The answer depends on factors such as budget, scalability, maintenance requirements, and control over data distribution.

Building Your Own CDN requires investing in a network of geographically distributed servers, setting up caching mechanisms, and managing load balancing. While this approach provides **full control over content distribution, security, and performance optimization**, it is highly complex and expensive. Only large-scale video platforms, such as Netflix and YouTube, typically develop proprietary CDN infrastructures to meet their unique performance demands.

On the other hand, **using a third-party CDN service** allows businesses to take advantage of an existing global network of optimized servers without the need for infrastructure management. Leading CDN providers like **Cloudflare, AWS CloudFront, and Akamai** offer extensive networks, advanced caching mechanisms, DDoS protection, and real-time analytics to monitor streaming performance.

The table below provides a comparison between building a private CDN and using third-party services

Criteria	Building Your Own CDN	Using Third-Party CDN (Cloudflare, AWS, Akamai, etc.)
Cost	Very high (hardware, maintenance, network expansion)	Pay-as-you-go or subscription-based pricing
Scalability	Limited by in-house resources	Instantly scalable with global infrastructure
Control	Full control over content delivery	Limited control, depends on provider's policies
Security	Customizable security protocols	Built-in security, including DDoS protection
Maintenance	Requires in-house expertise	Managed by the provider
Performance Optimization	Requires manual fine-tuning	Automatically optimized for speed and efficiency

For most streaming businesses, **using third-party CDNs is the best choice** due to cost efficiency, ease of setup, and high reliability. However, platforms with extreme performance needs and financial resources may consider developing their own CDN infrastructure.

CDN Performance for Faster Video Delivery

A well-optimized CDN ensures that video content reaches users quickly, with minimal buffering and high visual quality. To maximize performance, **caching mechanisms, content replication strategies, and data routing techniques must be implemented effectively**.

One of the key optimization techniques is **edge caching**, where video content is stored at CDN edge servers in multiple locations. When a user requests a video, the nearest edge server delivers the cached content instead of retrieving it from the origin server, reducing latency.

Another important aspect is **adaptive bitrate streaming (ABR)**, which dynamically adjusts video quality based on the user's network conditions. **Protocols such as HLS (HTTP Live Streaming) and DASH (Dynamic Adaptive Streaming over HTTP) work efficiently with a CDN**, ensuring seamless switching between different bitrate versions of a video.

Content prefetching is another technique that improves performance. Instead of waiting for a user request, a CDN can proactively **preload video files in high-traffic areas** based on predictive analytics. This ensures faster video start times, particularly for trending content.

To further optimize CDN performance, **geolocation-based routing** ensures that users are directed to the closest available server, reducing load times. Additionally, **persistent connections** using HTTP/2 or QUIC protocols reduce the overhead associated with repeated requests, improving overall streaming speed.

The following diagram explains the **workflow of an optimized CDN-based video streaming system**

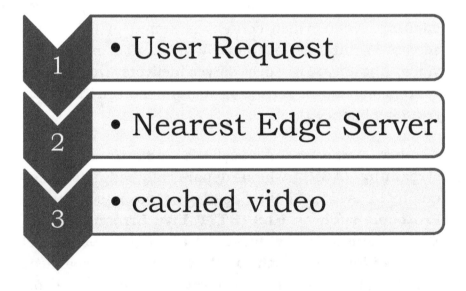

- User Request
- Nearest Edge Server
- cached video

Load Balancing and Edge Computing

A CDN not only improves speed but also ensures scalability by **distributing traffic across multiple edge servers**. Load balancing mechanisms **automatically redirect requests** to the least congested servers, preventing bottlenecks and ensuring smooth streaming even during peak hours.

Dynamic load balancing algorithms, such as round-robin and least connections, help distribute traffic intelligently. **Round-robin balancing** assigns incoming requests sequentially to available servers, while **least connections balancing** directs requests to the server with the lowest active connections, ensuring equal workload distribution.

Edge computing further improves scalability by processing certain tasks at the network's edge rather than at the origin server. Instead of merely caching static video files, **edge servers can handle real-time transcoding, analytics, and security enforcement**, reducing the processing burden on the core infrastructure.

This distributed approach allows video streaming platforms to **handle millions of concurrent users without service degradation**. The combination of **CDN, load balancing, and edge computing** ensures an efficient, scalable, and high-performance streaming experience.

Implementing a CDN is a crucial step in ensuring **fast, reliable, and scalable video streaming**. By distributing content across multiple geographically placed edge servers, a CDN **reduces latency, minimizes buffering, and improves bandwidth efficiency**.

Businesses must decide whether to **build their own CDN or use third-party providers such as Cloudflare, AWS CloudFront, or Akamai**. While a private CDN offers complete control, it is expensive and complex to manage. Third-party CDNs, on the other hand, provide a cost-effective and scalable solution. To optimize performance, techniques such as **edge caching, adaptive bitrate streaming, and geolocation-based routing** should be implemented. Additionally, **load balancing and edge computing** play a crucial role in handling high traffic loads while maintaining seamless video delivery. By carefully designing and optimizing CDN infrastructure, streaming platforms can **provide a superior viewing experience, improve content availability, and scale effortlessly to meet global demand**.

Chapter 6

Frontend Development – Video Player & UI

A video player is the **primary interface between the user and the content** in a video streaming platform. It is responsible for rendering video files, handling playback controls, and providing an intuitive user experience. The choice of a video player affects **streaming performance, customization options, compatibility with different devices, and support for various formats and streaming protocols**.

Modern streaming platforms rely on **HTML5-based video players**, which provide **native support across web browsers, mobile devices, and smart TVs** without requiring additional plugins. Popular video player frameworks such as **Video.js, Plyr, and custom-built HTML5 players** offer a wide range of customization and integration options.

The key factors when selecting a video player include **support for adaptive bitrate streaming, compatibility with multiple formats (MP4, HLS, DASH), playback controls, accessibility features (subtitles, closed captions), and responsiveness across different screen sizes**.

The diagram below illustrates the architecture of a **frontend video player in a streaming platform**

Choosing the Right Video Player

A streaming platform can either **use a third-party open-source video player** or **develop a custom-built player** based on HTML5.

The table below compares the most widely used video players for frontend development

Feature	HTML5 Video Player	Video.js	Plyr
Customization	Limited	Extensive	Moderate
Support for	Requires external	Built-in	Built-in

Feature	HTML5 Video Player	Video.js	Plyr
HLS/DASH	plugins	support	support
Cross-Browser Compatibility	High	High	High
Built-in UI/UX improvements	Basic	Advanced	Modern & lightweight
Plugin & API Support	Minimal	Extensive	Moderate
Mobile Responsiveness	Good	Excellent	Excellent

HTML5 video player is the simplest option and works well for basic video streaming needs. However, for more **advanced features like adaptive bitrate streaming, custom playback controls, and analytics tracking**, **Video.js** or **Plyr** are better choices due to their **extensive API support and modern UI elements**.

Customizing the UI/UX of the Video Player

A **well-designed user interface (UI) and user experience (UX) are critical for engaging viewers**

and ensuring smooth navigation. Customizing the video player allows streaming platforms to **align the design with their brand identity, improve accessibility, and improve interaction**.

Key customization elements include

- **Theming and styling the player** to match the platform's branding
- **Configuring playback controls**, such as play, pause, volume, and fullscreen options
- **Customizing loading animations and buffering indicators**
- **Adding interactive elements**, such as like/dislike buttons, comments, and playlists

Customizing a video player using **CSS and JavaScript** enables full control over the look and feel. The following example demonstrates **basic CSS styling for a Video.js player**

```
.video-js {
   background-color  #000;
   border-radius  8px;
}

.vjs-control-bar {
   background  rgba(0, 0, 0, 0.7);
}

.vjs-play-control {
   color  #ffffff;
```

}

For more advanced UI improvements, JavaScript-based event handling can be implemented. The following script dynamically **changes the theme of a Video.js player**

```
var player = videojs('my-video');

player.on('play', function() {
    console.log("Video started playing");
    player.addClass('custom-theme');
});
```

Implementing Playback Controls, Captions, and Subtitles

Playback controls are essential for a seamless user experience. A modern video player should support

- **Basic controls** (play, pause, stop, seek, volume adjustment)
- **Advanced controls** (playback speed, quality selection, picture-in-picture mode)
- **Keyboard shortcuts** for better accessibility
- **Gesture controls** for mobile devices

Adding **subtitles and closed captions** improves accessibility for viewers who are deaf or hard of hearing and improves engagement for multilingual audiences. Popular subtitle formats include **SRT**

(SubRip Subtitle) and VTT (WebVTT), which are widely supported by video players.

The following example demonstrates how to **embed subtitles into an HTML5 video player**

```
<video controls>
   <source src="video.mp4" type="video/mp4">
   <track   src="subtitles.vtt"   kind="subtitles"   srclang="en"
label="English">
</video>
```

For streaming platforms that support **multiple subtitle languages**, an API-based solution allows users to **dynamically switch between different subtitle files** without reloading the page.

Ensuring Cross-Device Compatibility

A key challenge in frontend development for video streaming platforms is **ensuring that the video player works seamlessly across multiple devices**. Users may access content on

- **Web browsers (Chrome, Firefox, Safari, Edge)**
- **Mobile devices (iOS, Android)**
- **Smart TVs and set-top boxes**

Cross-device compatibility is achieved through

- **Responsive design** that adapts the UI to different screen sizes
- **Adaptive bitrate streaming (HLS, DASH) for varying network conditions**
- **Progressive improvement techniques to ensure older devices can still access basic video playback features**

The table below summarizes the **compatibility of different video streaming technologies** across devices

Technology	Web Browsers	Mobile (iOS, Android)	Smart TVs
HTML5 Video	Yes	Yes	Limited
HLS (HTTP Live Streaming)	Yes (Safari native)	Yes	Yes
DASH (Dynamic Adaptive Streaming)	Yes	Yes	Yes
RTMP (Real-Time Messaging Protocol)	No	Limited	No
WebRTC (Real-Time Communication)	Yes	Yes	Limited

To **improve mobile performance, native app integration** is often required. **React Native Video and**

ExoPlayer are popular frameworks for embedding video players in iOS and Android applications.

The following diagram illustrates the **multi-device compatibility workflow for a video streaming platform**

A well-designed video player is a **fundamental aspect of a streaming platform's frontend development**. Choosing the right video player—whether HTML5, Video.js, or Plyr—ensures compatibility with various streaming formats, while UI customization improves the user experience.

Key features such as **playback controls, subtitles, and multi-device compatibility** improve accessibility and engagement. Ensuring **responsive design and**

adaptive bitrate streaming allows video content to be delivered smoothly across web, mobile, and smart TVs. By implementing **a robust video player with an intuitive UI, optimized playback controls, and seamless cross-device compatibility**, streaming platforms can **provide users with a high-quality viewing experience while maintaining efficiency and scalability**.

Chapter 7

Backend Development – User Management & Authentication

A **video streaming platform** is not just about delivering content; it also requires a **robust user management system** that ensures seamless authentication, secure access, and personalized experiences. The backend of a streaming service must handle **user registration, authentication, role-based access control, subscription management, and user data storage** efficiently. Without a well-structured authentication system, a platform is vulnerable to security threats such as unauthorized access, content piracy, and account hijacking.

For a streaming platform, authentication mechanisms such as **OAuth, JWT, and API keys** provide secure ways for users to sign in, while **role-based access control (RBAC)** ensures that different users have appropriate permissions based on their subscription level. **Subscription models and monetization strategies** determine how the platform generates revenue, whether through **pay-per-view, ad-based content, or premium access**. Additionally, **storing user data and watch history** enables personalized recommendations, content tracking, and a better user experience.

The diagram below provides an overview of the **user authentication and management flow** in a streaming platform

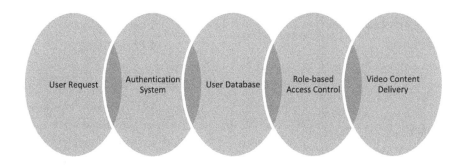

Setting Up User Authentication (OAuth, JWT, API Keys)

Authentication is the first step in securing a streaming platform. Users must sign in to access content, and their identity must be verified using **secure authentication mechanisms**.

The most commonly used authentication methods in modern web applications include

Authentication Method	Description	Use Case in Streaming
OAuth 2.0	A widely used open authentication standard that allows users to sign in using third-party services like Google, Facebook, or Apple.	Ideal for platforms that want quick sign-ins via social media and third-party services.

Authentication Method	Description	Use Case in Streaming
JWT (JSON Web Tokens)	A compact, URL-safe token-based authentication mechanism that securely transmits user identity and session data.	Best for API-driven authentication in mobile apps and SPAs (Single Page Applications).
API Keys	Unique keys assigned to users or applications for authentication and access control.	Used for machine-to-machine authentication and internal API security.

OAuth allows users to authenticate via **external identity providers** (Google, Facebook, Apple), simplifying login while offloading security responsibilities to these trusted providers. The OAuth workflow involves

1. The user clicks **"Sign in with Google"** on the streaming platform.
2. They are redirected to Google's authentication page.
3. After logging in, Google generates an **OAuth token** and sends it back to the platform.
4. The platform verifies the token and grants access.

JWT, on the other hand, provides a **stateless authentication mechanism**, which means that once a user logs in, their **JWT token** can be used for multiple requests without querying the database. This improves **performance and scalability**.

API keys are mainly used for **server-to-server authentication**, ensuring that only authorized applications or services can interact with the backend.

The following diagram illustrates the **JWT authentication process** in a streaming platform

Role-Based Access Control

A **streaming platform often has multiple types of users**, such as free users, premium subscribers, content creators, and administrators. Role-based access control (RBAC) ensures that each user has access only to the content and features that match their role.

RBAC implementation involves

1. **User Role Assignment** – When a user registers, they are assigned a role (e.g., free user, premium subscriber, admin).
2. **Content Permission System** – Content is tagged with permissions based on the assigned user roles.
3. **Access Validation** – Whenever a user requests a video, the system checks their role and grants or denies access accordingly.

The table below demonstrates how RBAC works in a streaming platform

User Role	Access Level
Free User	Limited access to selected free content, must watch ads.
Premium Subscriber	Full access to all content, no ads.

User Role	Access Level
Content Creator	Can upload and manage their own content.
Administrator	Full control over users, content, and platform settings.

For example, when a **premium subscriber** tries to watch a **premium movie**, the system validates their subscription before granting access. However, if a **free user** attempts the same action, they may be redirected to a subscription page or shown advertisements instead.

The following diagram illustrates **how RBAC controls access to content**

Subscription Models and Monetization

A streaming platform can generate revenue through various monetization models. The choice of a business model depends on the **target audience, content strategy, and market trends**.

The most common **monetization models for video streaming platforms** include

Monetization Model	Description	Examples
Subscription-Based (SVOD)	Users pay a monthly or yearly fee for unlimited access to content.	Netflix, Disney+
Pay-Per-View (TVOD)	Users pay for individual movies or events.	Amazon Prime Video (rentals)
Ad-Supported (AVOD)	Free content with advertisements generating revenue.	YouTube, Pluto TV
Hybrid Model	Combination of subscription and ad-supported content.	Hulu, Peacock

SVOD provides **predictable revenue streams** but requires high-quality exclusive content to retain subscribers. TVOD is suitable for **live events or exclusive movie rentals**. AVOD is **free to users** but relies on advertisements for revenue. Implementing a **payment gateway (Stripe, PayPal, Razorpay) and subscription management system** is essential for handling transactions, renewals, and cancellations.

Storing User Data and Video Watch History

To **improve user experience and provide personalized recommendations**, a streaming platform must store **user data, watch history, and viewing preferences**.

Key data points stored in the database include

- **User profile details** (name, email, subscription status)
- **Watch history** (videos watched, timestamps)
- **Viewing preferences** (preferred genres, watchlist)
- **Interaction data** (likes, comments, shares)

The table below shows an example of how user watch history can be stored

User ID	Video Title	Timestamp	Watch Duration	Status
1001	The Dark	2025-03-10	1hr 45min	Completed

User ID	Video Title	Timestamp	Watch Duration	Status
	Knight	20 30		
1002	Stranger Things S1E1	2025-03-11 15 00	32min	In Progress

This data is then **used by recommendation algorithms** to suggest content based on **watch patterns, preferences, and engagement levels**.

A typical **user data storage architecture** looks like this

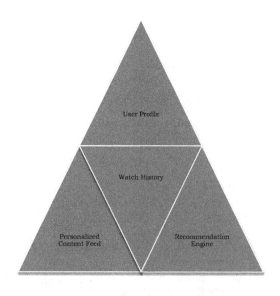

For scalability, **NoSQL databases (MongoDB, Firebase)** are commonly used due to their ability to handle large volumes of user data efficiently. User authentication and management are **critical components** of a video streaming platform. Implementing **OAuth, JWT, and API keys** ensures secure and seamless user authentication, while **role-based access control (RBAC)** protects content by defining different user roles. Monetization models like **subscription-based, pay-per-view, and ad-supported streaming** define how revenue is generated. Storing user watch history and preferences helps in delivering a **personalized viewing experience**. By using **secure authentication, scalable user data storage, and advanced monetization strategies**, a streaming platform can **improve security, improve user engagement, and maximize revenue potential**.

Chapter 8

Video Storage and Database Management

A video streaming platform handles large volumes of **video files, metadata, and user interactions**, requiring a **robust storage and database management system**. The choice of **storage solution** plays a crucial role in determining **scalability, performance, and cost efficiency**. Efficient **database structuring and indexing mechanisms** further improve the platform's ability to quickly retrieve and manage video content.

When designing a storage and database system for a streaming service, several critical aspects must be considered, including **how video files are stored, how metadata is structured, how videos are indexed for quick searching, and how caching mechanisms are implemented to improve performance**. By optimizing these factors, a platform can ensure **seamless content delivery, reduced latency, and efficient data retrieval** for an optimal user experience.

Choosing a Storage Solution

Selecting the right storage solution is crucial because videos require significant storage space, high-speed access, and global availability. The choice between **cloud-based storage solutions and self-hosted local storage** depends on factors like **cost, scalability, and ease of access**.

The most commonly used **video storage solutions** include

Storage Solution	Description	Best For
AWS S3 (Amazon Simple Storage Service)	A highly scalable cloud storage solution offering secure, durable, and cost-effective storage for video streaming platforms.	Large-scale streaming services needing global content delivery and scalability.
Google Cloud Storage	A high-performance cloud storage service with built-in AI capabilities for metadata analysis and optimization.	AI-powered recommendations and real-time analytics for video platforms.
Local NAS (Network-Attached Storage)	A self-hosted solution where videos are stored on local network drives for quick access.	Small-scale platforms looking for **low-cost, in-house storage** solutions.

Cloud-based solutions like **AWS S3 and Google Cloud Storage** provide **global scalability and durability**, ensuring that video files are stored securely and accessible worldwide. On the other hand, **NAS solutions** offer a **cheaper alternative for small-scale platforms** but lack the ability to handle millions of simultaneous requests efficiently.

A **hybrid storage model**, where frequently accessed videos are cached locally while rarely accessed videos are stored in the cloud, provides a **cost-effective balance between performance and scalability**.

Structuring a Database for Video Metadata

Efficient database structuring ensures **fast retrieval, easy categorization, and improved searchability of video content**. A well-designed database schema must store essential **video metadata**, including **title, description, duration, resolution, genre, upload date, and user engagement statistics**.

The choice between **relational (SQL) and non-relational (NoSQL) databases** depends on the platform's needs.

Database Type	Description	Best For
MySQL / PostgreSQL	Structured data storage with	Platforms requiring **structured metadata**

Database Type	Description	Best For
(Relational DBs)	predefined schema, ensuring consistency and reliability.	**with strict relationships** (e.g., user subscriptions, video categories).
MongoDB (NoSQL Database)	Schema-less, document-based storage, allowing flexible metadata storage and fast retrieval.	Platforms handling **large-scale unstructured metadata, user interactions, and recommendations**.

A **relational database (MySQL or PostgreSQL)** is ideal for **structured video metadata**, such as **user accounts, subscriptions, and payment records**, whereas a **NoSQL database like MongoDB** is better suited for **dynamic metadata, user-generated content, and recommendation algorithms**.

The following **database schema example** demonstrates how a relational database stores video metadata in **MySQL**

```
CREATE TABLE videos (
    video_id INT PRIMARY KEY AUTO_INCREMENT,
    title VARCHAR(255) NOT NULL,
    description TEXT,
    duration INT,
```

```
    resolution VARCHAR(50),
    upload_date TIMESTAMP DEFAULT CURRENT_TIMESTAMP,
    genre VARCHAR(100),
    views INT DEFAULT 0,
    likes INT DEFAULT 0
);
```

For a **NoSQL (MongoDB) database**, a video metadata document might look like this

```
{
    "video_id" "xyz123",
    "title" "Best Action Movie",
    "description" "An action-packed movie with thrilling scenes.",
    "duration" 7200,
    "resolution" "1080p",
    "upload_date" "2025-03-12T10 30 00Z",
    "genre" ["Action", "Thriller"],
    "views" 500000,
    "likes" 45000
}
```

A **hybrid approach**, where **SQL is used for structured data and NoSQL is used for flexible metadata storage**, provides the best of both worlds.

Indexing and Searching for Video Content

A **video streaming platform must allow users to search for videos quickly**, requiring **efficient indexing and search optimization techniques**.

To improve search performance, indexing is applied to key metadata fields such as **title, genre, tags, and upload date**.

Indexing Method	Description	Use Case
Full-Text Search (SQL Indexing)	Speeds up searching through text fields such as video titles and descriptions.	Searching for videos based on **keywords**.
ElasticSearch (NoSQL Search Engine)	Provides real-time, scalable search capabilities with auto-suggestions.	Large-scale video streaming services with **millions of search queries**.
Tag-Based Indexing	Organizes videos based on **categories, genres, and trending topics**.	Personalized recommendations and trending video sections.

An optimized search **reduces database load**, ensuring **fast content discovery** for users.

The following SQL query demonstrates **how indexing improves search performance**

```
CREATE INDEX idx_title ON videos (title);
SELECT * FROM videos WHERE title LIKE '%action%';
```

By using **ElasticSearch**, the platform can **handle millions of queries per second** with real-time suggestions and personalized search results.

Caching Mechanisms for Better Performance

Caching is an essential technique for improving **video streaming performance** and reducing **server load**. By **storing frequently accessed data in temporary storage**, caching eliminates the need for repeated database queries, resulting in **faster load times** and **smoother playback**.

There are three primary types of caching mechanisms used in video streaming platforms

Caching Type	Description	Best Use Case
CDN Caching	Stores video content on geographically distributed servers for faster delivery.	Streaming platforms with **global users requiring low latency**.
Database Query Caching (Redis, Memcached)	Caches frequently queried metadata to reduce database	Platforms handling **millions of metadata**

Caching Type	Description	Best Use Case
	load.	**requests**.
Local Browser Caching	Temporarily stores video chunks on the user's device for seamless playback.	Improving **buffering speed and playback smoothness**.

A **CDN (Content Delivery Network)** caches **video files closer to users**, while **Redis or Memcached** caches **video metadata** for faster retrieval. The combination of **CDN + database caching** ensures **both video content and metadata are delivered with minimal latency**.

Efficient **video storage and database management** are essential for **scalability, speed, and cost optimization** in a streaming platform. The choice of **cloud-based vs. local storage**, combined with **structured (SQL) and unstructured (NoSQL) database solutions**, determines how well the platform handles **large-scale video content**. Implementing **advanced indexing and caching mechanisms** ensures **fast search performance, seamless playback, and reduced server load**. By using **hybrid storage solutions, optimized search indexing, and caching strategies**, a video streaming platform can deliver high-quality content efficiently while maintaining cost-effectiveness and scalability.

Chapter 9

Live Streaming and Real-Time Interaction

Live streaming has revolutionized digital content consumption by allowing real-time video broadcasting to audiences worldwide. Unlike traditional on-demand streaming, which relies on pre-recorded content stored in a media server, live streaming involves continuous data transmission, enabling viewers to watch events as they happen. This dynamic method of content delivery is widely used for broadcasting sports events, concerts, gaming sessions, corporate webinars, and interactive online classes.

A successful live streaming setup requires a well-integrated infrastructure comprising a **live streaming server, encoding tools, content distribution networks (CDNs), and real-time engagement mechanisms**. The key challenges in live streaming include ensuring low latency, maintaining high video quality, handling large-scale concurrent viewers, and incorporating interactive features like live chat, reactions, and real-time analytics.

Setting Up a Live Streaming Server

A live streaming server acts as the **intermediary between the video source and the end-users**, handling video ingestion, processing, and distribution. Popular live streaming servers include **Wowza Streaming Engine, Red5, Ant Media Server, and Nginx RTMP module**. Each offers unique advantages in terms of scalability, protocol support, and integration capabilities.

The setup process generally involves the following steps

Configuring the server The streaming server must be installed on a dedicated machine or a cloud-based virtual server with sufficient bandwidth and processing power.

Enabling RTMP (Real-Time Messaging Protocol) ingestion Most live streaming setups use **RTMP** for transmitting video from the source to the server, where it is then converted into HLS (HTTP Live Streaming) or DASH (Dynamic Adaptive Streaming over HTTP) for efficient content delivery.

Encoding and transcoding Live video streams must be encoded into a suitable format using **H.264, VP9, or H.265 codecs** before being distributed to viewers. The server performs additional transcoding to generate multiple resolutions for adaptive bitrate streaming.

Integrating with a CDN To ensure smooth and scalable distribution, the streaming server relays the live feed to a CDN, which caches and delivers the stream to users worldwide with minimal delay.

The following table compares **popular live streaming servers**

Streaming Server	Features	Best Use Case	Supported Protocols
Wowza Streaming Engine	Highly scalable, adaptive bitrate streaming	Large-scale enterprise live streaming	RTMP, HLS, DASH, WebRTC
Red5 Server	Open-source, cost-effective	Community-driven live streaming	RTMP, WebRTC
Ant Media Server	Low-latency WebRTC support	Interactive live streaming	WebRTC, RTMP, HLS
Nginx RTMP Module	Lightweight and easy to configure	Basic live streaming setups	RTMP

Streaming from Different Sources

Live streaming can originate from multiple sources, including **OBS (Open Broadcaster Software), mobile devices, webcams, and hardware encoders**.

OBS is one of the most widely used open-source software solutions for live streaming, offering real-time audio and video capture with customizable scenes, overlays, and bitrate settings. For professional broadcasts, hardware encoders like **Blackmagic Web Presenter** or **Teradek Vidiu** provide **higher-quality streams with minimal latency**.

The process of streaming from **OBS Studio** involves

Configuring the stream settings Users need to enter the RTMP server URL and stream key provided by the streaming server or platform.

Setting up video and audio sources OBS allows adding multiple input sources such as webcams, screen captures, and external audio devices.

Adjusting bitrate and resolution To balance quality and network efficiency, an appropriate bitrate must be selected based on available bandwidth.

Starting the live stream Once the setup is complete, clicking the "Start Streaming" button sends the live feed to the streaming server.

For mobile-based live streaming, apps like **Streamlabs, Larix Broadcaster, and Facebook Live Producer** enable users to stream directly using their phone cameras. These applications integrate with RTMP servers and CDNs, offering flexibility for on-the-go broadcasting.

Handling Live Chat, Reactions and Analytics

A major advantage of live streaming over traditional broadcasting is the ability to incorporate real-time **interaction features** such as live chat, reactions (likes, emojis, shares), and real-time analytics.

Live chat enables viewers to communicate with the broadcaster and other audience members, fostering engagement. Implementing a scalable chat system involves **WebSockets** or **Socket.IO** for bidirectional communication between clients and the server.

Reactions and engagement features such as "likes" or animated emojis improve viewer participation. These are typically implemented using **event-driven WebSockets** or **server-sent events (SSEs)** to provide real-time updates without excessive server load.

Real-time analytics track crucial streaming metrics, including concurrent viewers, watch duration, buffering rates, and geographic distribution of audiences. Advanced streaming platforms integrate **Google Analytics, AWS Kinesis, or proprietary machine learning models** to generate insights for optimizing content and improving user experience.

The following table summarizes key **real-time interaction components**

Feature	Implementation Technology	Purpose
Live Chat	WebSockets, Socket.IO	Enables real-time viewer interaction
Reactions (likes, emojis, etc.)	WebSockets, SSE	improves engagement
Real-time Analytics	Google Analytics, AWS Kinesis	Provides performance insights

Low-Latency Streaming Techniques

One of the primary challenges in live streaming is **reducing latency**, which is the delay between video capture and playback on the user's device. Traditional HLS-based streaming introduces latency of **10 to 30 seconds**, which can be problematic for interactive broadcasts. To minimize delays, several low-latency streaming technologies have been developed

WebRTC (Web Real-Time Communication) A protocol designed for peer-to-peer streaming with sub-second latency. It is ideal for interactive live streams such as video conferencing and gaming.

LL-HLS (Low-Latency HLS) An improvement to traditional HLS, reducing latency to 2-5 seconds while maintaining scalability through CDN support.

RTMP with Low Latency Adjustments By fine-tuning RTMP parameters, latency can be reduced to approximately 3-5 seconds, making it suitable for **live auctions, gaming streams, and interactive broadcasts**.

Choosing the right **low-latency technique** depends on the type of live stream. **WebRTC is best for interactive sessions**, while **LL-HLS provides a balance between low latency and CDN scalability**. Live streaming is a powerful way to **engage audiences in real time**, requiring a **well-structured architecture** that includes a **live streaming server, video sources, encoding tools, and a CDN** for global distribution. Interactive features such as **live chat, reactions, and analytics** play a critical role in enhancing user engagement, while **low-latency streaming technologies** like WebRTC and LL-HLS ensure near-instant video delivery. By using the right combination of **streaming protocols, server configurations, and engagement tools**, a live streaming platform can **deliver high-quality, real-time content to viewers worldwide while maintaining scalability and performance**.

Chapter 10

Security and Digital Rights Management (DRM)

As the demand for digital content grows, so does the risk of piracy, unauthorized access, and content theft. Protecting video content is crucial for businesses and content creators who monetize their streaming services. Without proper security measures, copyrighted material can be illegally downloaded, redistributed, or even restreamed to unauthorized audiences, leading to **revenue loss, legal complications, and brand damage**.

To combat piracy, various **Digital Rights Management (DRM) systems, encryption techniques, and access control mechanisms** are employed to ensure only authorized users can view the content. These measures prevent unauthorized downloads, **stream ripping, credential sharing, and hacking attempts** that target video streaming platforms.

The security architecture of a robust streaming service typically involves **DRM implementation, video encryption, tokenized access, and forensic watermarking**, along with **monitoring tools to detect and block suspicious activities**.

The following diagram illustrates the **video security workflow**

Video Content

DRM Protection

Encryption

CDN Delivery

Authorized Viewer

Protecting Video Content from Piracy

Video piracy is a significant issue affecting streaming services, online educational platforms, and live event broadcasters. The most common methods of content piracy include **stream ripping, screen recording, illegal redistribution, and credential sharing**. To effectively protect video content, a multi-layered security approach must be implemented.

One of the primary techniques for preventing unauthorized access is **Tokenized URL Authentication**, where video playback is restricted using time-limited access tokens. These tokens are generated dynamically and are unique to each session, ensuring that **video links cannot be shared or**

reused. Another essential measure is **AES-128 encryption**, which scrambles video files so they can only be decrypted by authorized users with a valid decryption key. This ensures that even if video files are intercepted during transmission, they remain unusable without proper authentication.

The following table summarizes **common video piracy methods and countermeasures**

Piracy Method	Description	Countermeasure
Stream Ripping	Capturing video streams using third-party tools	DRM, encryption, tokenized access
Screen Recording	Recording screen playback	Watermarking, device restriction
Credential Sharing	Users sharing login details	Multi-factor authentication (MFA), IP restriction
Illegal Redistribution	Unauthorized re-hosting of content	Watermarking, tracking digital fingerprints

Implementing DRM Solutions

Digital Rights Management (DRM) is a technology used to **control access to digital content, restrict unauthorized copying, and enforce licensing policies**. DRM solutions are essential for securing premium video content and are required by major streaming platforms, including **Netflix, Disney+, and Amazon Prime Video**.

There are three widely used DRM systems, each designed for compatibility with specific platforms

Google Widevine Used for securing video content on **Android devices, Chrome browsers, and smart TVs**.

Apple FairPlay The preferred DRM for **iOS devices, Safari browsers, and Apple TV**.

Microsoft PlayReady Commonly used for **Windows-based platforms, Edge browser, and Xbox consoles**.

The implementation of DRM involves **encrypting the video file and licensing it through a DRM server**, which issues decryption keys only to authenticated users. This ensures that even if a video file is downloaded, it cannot be played without proper authorization.

The following table provides an overview of **popular DRM solutions and their compatibility**

DRM Solution	Supported Platforms	Best Use Case
Google Widevine	Android, Chrome, Smart TVs	Secure streaming on mobile and web
Apple FairPlay	iOS, Safari, Apple TV	Protecting Apple ecosystem content
Microsoft PlayReady	Windows, Edge, Xbox	DRM for enterprise-level security

A typical **DRM workflow** consists of the following steps

1. **Encryption** The video file is encrypted using DRM-compatible protection during encoding.
2. **License Server Communication** When a user requests to play the video, the player sends a request to the **DRM license server**.
3. **User Authentication** The DRM server verifies whether the user has the right permissions to access the content.
4. **Decryption and Playback** If authorized, the server sends a decryption key to the player, allowing playback.

Secure Video Encryption

In addition to DRM, **video encryption** plays a crucial role in preventing unauthorized access. **AES-128 encryption** is widely used in video streaming, particularly for **HLS (HTTP Live Streaming)**, to secure content before delivery.

Encrypted video streaming involves the following steps

- **Encryption During Encoding** The video file is encrypted using AES-128, generating a unique key for decryption.
- **Key Storage in a Secure Server** The decryption key is stored separately on a **key management server (KMS)**.
- **Token-Based Access Control** Each playback request is validated using an authentication token to ensure that only authorized users can retrieve the decryption key.

Token-based access can be implemented using **JWT (JSON Web Tokens)**, ensuring that playback links are time-sensitive and cannot be reused. For example, a token might expire after **15 minutes**, preventing link-sharing and unauthorized distribution.

The following table outlines **encryption techniques used in video streaming**

Encryption Method	Usage	Security Level
AES-128 Encryption	HLS streaming	High
RSA Public-Key Encryption	DRM key exchange	Very High
TLS (Transport Layer Security)	Secure data transmission	Medium

Preventing Stream Ripping

Even with DRM and encryption, some users attempt to **rip video streams** using tools that capture network traffic or record the screen. To counter this, additional security measures must be in place.

One effective technique is **Watermarking**, where an **invisible or visible identifier** is embedded into the video. This helps trace illegally shared content back to the original user.

Another approach is **blocking unauthorized video capture tools**, which can be achieved by

- **Disabling screen recording on mobile devices** using system-level APIs.

- **Blocking browser extensions** that capture streams by monitoring network requests.
- **Using forensic watermarking** to track and identify pirated content.

Forensic watermarking embeds **unique user-specific information** within each video stream, allowing rights holders to identify the source of a leak even if the content is re-recorded or modified.

The following table highlights **common anti-piracy techniques**

Anti-Piracy Technique	Implementation	Effectiveness
Tokenized URLs	Time-sensitive authentication	High
Forensic Watermarking	User-specific hidden identifiers	Very High
Blocking Screen Recording	System-level API restrictions	Moderate

Security is a **critical aspect of video streaming**, ensuring that content creators, media companies, and platforms **retain control over their intellectual property**. By implementing **DRM solutions such as**

Widevine, FairPlay, and PlayReady, streaming services can prevent unauthorized access and piracy. Encryption techniques such as **AES-128 and RSA key exchange** add another layer of protection, while **tokenized access and forensic watermarking** safeguard against unauthorized sharing. Combining **multi-layered encryption, DRM policies, and proactive monitoring** ensures that video content remains secure, preventing financial losses due to piracy. By using these advanced security measures, streaming platforms can **build a sustainable, protected digital ecosystem while maintaining a seamless user experience**.

Chapter 11

Performance Optimization and Scaling

One of the key challenges faced by video streaming platforms is ensuring smooth, uninterrupted video delivery to users, especially during periods of high traffic or on networks with varying bandwidth capacities. The quality of the user experience is paramount in the competitive world of streaming services, where even a small interruption or delay can lead to a loss of viewers. To overcome these challenges, platforms must employ various **performance optimization** techniques, along with the ability to **scale infrastructure** to meet the demands of users across the globe. In this chapter, we will explore effective ways to **reduce video buffering**, optimize **server load**, utilize **AI-based recommendations**, and **scale infrastructure** efficiently to handle high traffic loads.

Techniques for Reducing Video Buffering

Video buffering is one of the most common frustrations for viewers, leading to interrupted playback and a negative viewing experience. Buffering occurs when the video player has not loaded enough data to continue playback smoothly, forcing the player to pause and reload. To mitigate this, video streaming platforms need to focus on both the **pre-buffering of video data** and the **effective management of streaming protocols**.

The first technique to consider is **adaptive bitrate streaming** (ABS). ABS dynamically adjusts the quality of the video stream based on the user's available bandwidth. For example, when a user's internet speed fluctuates, the platform can switch between higher and lower bitrate versions of the video to ensure smooth playback. This can be achieved using protocols like **HLS** (HTTP Live Streaming) and **DASH** (Dynamic Adaptive Streaming over HTTP). These protocols break the video into chunks, each chunk encoded at multiple bitrates. When the player detects a drop in bandwidth, it can switch to a lower bitrate without interrupting playback.

Another technique to minimize buffering is **preloading**. In this process, the video player loads a portion of the video before the viewer presses play. This allows the player to begin playback immediately, with the initial chunks of video already in the buffer. Preloading is particularly effective when combined with **content delivery networks (CDNs)**, which distribute video files across multiple edge servers close to the user's location, reducing the time required for data to travel.

Finally, **buffer size optimization** plays a role in buffering prevention. Adjusting the buffer size based on network conditions ensures that the video player maintains an optimal amount of preloaded data. If the buffer is too small, the user might experience interruptions, but if it's too large, the video player could waste bandwidth unnecessarily. Finding the right balance is critical to minimize buffering while maintaining efficiency.

Optimizing Server Load and Bandwidth Usage

In video streaming, **server load** and **bandwidth usage** are directly linked to the amount of content being delivered and the number of viewers. High-quality video streams, especially those delivered in high resolution (such as 4K), demand significant server resources and bandwidth. To maintain performance while minimizing costs, streaming platforms must optimize both the server load and the bandwidth used during video delivery.

One of the most effective techniques is the use of **Content Delivery Networks (CDNs)**. CDNs improve performance by caching video content on **edge servers** located closer to the user. When a viewer requests a video, the CDN serves the content from the nearest edge server, drastically reducing the amount of bandwidth required for long-distance data transfer. This reduces latency, speeds up the delivery process, and offloads traffic from the main server.

Another important optimization technique is **load balancing**. Load balancing involves distributing incoming traffic across multiple servers to prevent any one server from being overwhelmed. This ensures that each server handles a manageable amount of traffic, which prevents slowdowns or service outages during periods of high demand. Load balancing can be done at both the **application layer** and the **network layer**. **Application-level load balancing** routes requests to servers based on factors like server capacity, while **network-level load balancing** uses DNS or IP address routing to direct users to the best available server.

To further optimize bandwidth usage, **video compression techniques** can be applied. **H.265/HEVC (High-Efficiency Video Coding)** is a newer video codec that compresses video data more efficiently than older codecs like **H.264**. By using more advanced encoding techniques, streaming services can deliver high-quality video while reducing the amount of data transmitted, thus saving bandwidth and improving overall system performance.

The following table compares various techniques for **optimizing server load and bandwidth usage**

Optimization Technique	Benefit	Key Technologies Used
Content Delivery Network (CDN)	Reduces server load by caching content closer to	Akamai, Cloudflare, AWS CloudFront

Optimization Technique	Benefit	Key Technologies Used
	users	
Load Balancing	Distributes traffic across multiple servers to avoid overloading	Nginx, HAProxy, Amazon ELB (Elastic Load Balancer)
Video Compression (HEVC/H.265)	Reduces the file size without sacrificing quality	H.265 codec, x265 encoder

Using AI-Based Recommendations

One of the most significant advantages of modern video streaming platforms is the ability to offer **personalized content recommendations**. These recommendations improve the user experience by helping viewers discover videos they are likely to enjoy based on their past viewing behavior, demographic data, and even real-time engagement.

AI and machine learning algorithms are at the core of content recommendation engines. These algorithms analyze **user behavior**, **viewing history**, and **interactions** to predict what type of content will most likely engage the user. Popular streaming services like

Netflix, YouTube, and Spotify use these systems to increase user engagement and reduce churn.

The recommendation process typically follows these steps

Data Collection User interaction data is collected, such as videos watched, time spent on each video, ratings, and search queries.

Data Processing AI algorithms process this data to identify patterns and preferences.

Prediction and Personalization The system predicts what videos will appeal to the user and creates a personalized queue or playlist.

Real-Time Adjustment As the user interacts with the platform, the recommendation engine continues to adjust in real-time, adapting to changes in user behavior.

Beyond recommendations, AI can also optimize video delivery. For instance, AI-based systems can adjust the video stream quality based on **real-time user engagement**. If a user skips videos frequently, the system may lower the stream quality to save bandwidth, while if the user watches videos for longer periods, the system may automatically improve the video quality for a better experience.

Infrastructure to Handle High Traffic Loads

As video streaming platforms gain more users, particularly during peak hours or live events, the ability to **scale infrastructure** becomes crucial. Properly scaling your infrastructure ensures that your platform can handle increasing user demand without compromising performance.

The process of scaling can be approached in two ways **vertical scaling** and **horizontal scaling**.

Vertical Scaling (Scaling Up) This involves adding more resources to a single server, such as upgrading CPU, RAM, or storage. While vertical scaling can work well for applications with lower traffic, it has limitations and may become cost-prohibitive as demand increases.

Horizontal Scaling (Scaling Out) This is the process of adding more servers to distribute the load. Horizontal scaling is a more flexible and scalable solution for video streaming services because it allows for the addition of servers as needed to handle the traffic load. **Load balancing** plays a critical role in horizontal scaling, as it ensures that traffic is evenly distributed across all available servers.

To support scalability, streaming platforms often use **cloud-based solutions**. Cloud platforms such as

Amazon Web Services (AWS), Google Cloud Platform (GCP), and Microsoft Azure provide dynamic scaling capabilities. Cloud services automatically adjust server capacity based on demand, ensuring that resources are available during high-traffic periods while minimizing costs during off-peak hours.

Another key consideration in scaling is the use of **distributed databases** and **object storage systems**. In a cloud environment, databases such as **Amazon RDS** or **Google Cloud SQL** can scale horizontally to support large numbers of concurrent users and provide high availability. For video storage, **object storage systems** like **Amazon S3** or **Google Cloud Storage** allow platforms to store large video files across multiple data centers, ensuring fast access and redundancy. The following diagram illustrates the process of **horizontal scaling with load balancing**

Optimizing video streaming performance and scaling infrastructure to meet the demands of high-traffic periods are essential for delivering an uninterrupted user experience. By implementing **adaptive bitrate streaming, reducing buffering**, and using techniques like **AI-based recommendations** and **video compression**, streaming services can improve the quality of their content delivery. Additionally, **scaling infrastructure** through **CDNs**, **load balancing**, and **cloud solutions** ensures that platforms can handle spikes in traffic while maintaining optimal performance. The ability to deliver **personalized, high-quality content** efficiently will determine the long-term success of a streaming platform. As technology continues to evolve, the future of video streaming will be increasingly reliant on **data-driven optimization and scalability**, offering users a seamless and engaging experience across any device or network condition.

Chapter 12

Deploying Your Video Streaming Platform

Deploying a video streaming platform involves much more than simply uploading content and configuring a media server. It requires a strategic approach to ensure that the platform is scalable, secure, and able to deliver high-quality video content to users with minimal interruptions. A successful deployment considers various hosting options, ensures smooth updates with a continuous integration and continuous deployment (CI/CD) pipeline, and incorporates robust monitoring and troubleshooting mechanisms to guarantee that everything runs smoothly. This chapter will provide an in-depth explanation of the deployment process, offering valuable insights on **hosting options**, **CI/CD setup**, **system monitoring**, and **maintenance best practices**.

Hosting Options for Video Streaming Platforms

When it comes to hosting your video streaming platform, there are several options to choose from, each with its own set of benefits and considerations. The choice of hosting depends largely on your specific needs, such as scalability, cost-efficiency, control over infrastructure, and performance. Below are the key hosting options available

Cloud Hosting AWS, Azure, and Google Cloud

Cloud hosting has become the go-to choice for most video streaming platforms due to its flexibility, scalability, and cost-effectiveness. Major cloud providers such as **Amazon Web Services (AWS)**, **Microsoft Azure**, and **Google Cloud Platform (GCP)** offer a wide range of services to support video streaming, including **content delivery networks (CDNs)**, **object storage systems**, **media processing tools**, and **virtual machines** for hosting backend services.

Amazon Web Services (AWS) AWS is a robust cloud platform that provides a variety of tools specifically designed for video streaming. For example, **AWS Elemental MediaLive** is a service for live video encoding, and **AWS MediaStore** provides scalable storage solutions for media content. Additionally, **AWS CloudFront** is a CDN that accelerates content delivery globally by caching video at edge locations. For storage, **Amazon S3** offers a secure, scalable storage solution for video files. The flexibility to pay only for what you use is an appealing aspect of AWS, making it a good option for scaling based on demand.

Microsoft Azure Azure also offers a range of services tailored for video streaming, such as **Azure Media Services**, which provides media encoding, packaging, and streaming services. Azure's CDN can deliver low-latency video streams to users worldwide, and Azure Blob Storage is a popular choice for storing large media files. Like AWS, Azure offers scalability and performance optimization, but it may be more suited for organizations already using Microsoft's ecosystem or for those requiring specific integrations with Azure's other enterprise services.

Google Cloud Platform (GCP) GCP provides a suite of services that cater to video streaming platforms. **Google Cloud Storage** is highly scalable and reliable for storing large media files, while **Google Cloud CDN** ensures fast video delivery with low latency. Google's data processing tools, such as **Google Cloud Video Intelligence API**, enable video indexing, allowing for easier search and categorization of content.

On-Premise Hosting

On-premise hosting is another option, although it comes with significant challenges. In an on-premise setup, you would have full control over the physical hardware and software, giving you the ability to customize every aspect of your infrastructure. However, managing an on-premise solution requires considerable expertise in networking, security, and hardware management.

One of the primary advantages of on-premise hosting is that you are not dependent on third-party cloud providers, which can be appealing for organizations that need full control over their infrastructure or are concerned about data security. On-premise hosting is also a viable option if you have sufficient resources and require a dedicated infrastructure for your streaming service.

However, there are notable drawbacks, such as higher upfront costs for purchasing servers and networking equipment, as well as the ongoing costs for maintenance and power. Additionally, scaling on-premise infrastructure can be difficult and costly, especially during peak traffic periods.

Setting Up CI/CD for Smooth Updates

The process of deploying a video streaming platform involves continuous updates, whether it's for new features, bug fixes, or performance improvements. A **CI/CD (Continuous Integration/Continuous Deployment)** pipeline is an essential part of modern software development, ensuring that changes are quickly integrated and deployed with minimal downtime and without affecting the user experience.

Continuous Integration (CI) refers to the practice of automatically integrating code changes into a shared repository several times a day. This practice allows developers to catch issues early in the development process, ensuring that the codebase remains stable.

Continuous Deployment (CD) automates the process of deploying these changes into the production environment. Once code passes all necessary tests and validation steps in the CI pipeline, it can be automatically deployed to production. This reduces the need for manual intervention, enabling faster releases and reducing the likelihood of human error.

For video streaming platforms, CI/CD pipelines typically involve several stages

Code Commit and Build Developers commit changes to a version control system (e.g., GitHub, GitLab). The code is then automatically compiled and tested.

Automated Testing A suite of automated tests, including unit tests, integration tests, and end-to-end tests, are executed to ensure that the code works as expected.

Staging Deployment After passing the tests, the application is deployed to a staging environment that mimics the production environment. This allows the team to catch any environment-specific issues.

Production Deployment Once everything is confirmed in staging, the application is deployed to the production servers. CI/CD tools like **Jenkins, GitLab CI, and CircleCI** can be used to automate this entire process.

Here's a simplified diagram illustrating a **CI/CD pipeline** for a video streaming platform

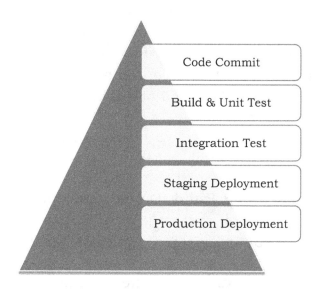

Code Commit

Build & Unit Test

Integration Test

Staging Deployment

Production Deployment

Implementing CI/CD ensures that updates to the platform are deployed quickly, securely, and with minimal risk of downtime or bugs affecting users.

Monitoring System Health and Troubleshooting

Monitoring the health of your video streaming platform is critical for ensuring that your service runs smoothly and is responsive to any issues. A robust monitoring system can help identify bottlenecks, detect failures, and provide insights into user behavior and system performance.

To effectively monitor system health, streaming platforms often rely on **application performance monitoring (APM)** tools and **infrastructure monitoring** systems. Popular tools include

New Relic Provides real-time insights into the performance of your application, including response times, error rates, and throughput. It also offers detailed analytics on how your video streaming platform is performing, which can help diagnose issues quickly.

Datadog Offers cloud monitoring and analytics for applications and infrastructure. It helps track key metrics, such as CPU usage, memory usage, and server health, and alerts you when thresholds are breached.

Prometheus and Grafana These open-source tools are widely used for monitoring and alerting. Prometheus collects metrics from your application, while Grafana provides visualization to help interpret these metrics.

Additionally, **log management** tools like **ELK Stack** (Elasticsearch, Logstash, and Kibana) are crucial for troubleshooting. Logs generated by the video servers, databases, and other components can be aggregated and analyzed to find the root cause of issues. These logs can include error messages, warnings, and performance data that can help in troubleshooting when issues arise.

Best Practices for Maintenance and Upgrades

Regular maintenance and planning for future upgrades are crucial for ensuring the long-term success of a video streaming platform. Some of the best practices include

Regular Software Updates Keeping your platform's software up-to-date is vital for ensuring security and performance. This includes updating operating systems, media servers, and application dependencies.

Automated Backups Video content and user data should be regularly backed up to ensure that you can recover from data loss in the event of hardware failure, cyber-attacks, or other unforeseen issues. Cloud services typically offer automated backup solutions that you can configure.

Load Testing Before scaling your infrastructure, conduct **load testing** to simulate high-traffic conditions and identify potential bottlenecks or weak points. This allows you to optimize the system before it goes live.

User Feedback Actively monitor user feedback and usage patterns. This information can help guide future platform updates, ensuring that the changes align with user expectations.

Capacity Planning As your platform grows, it is essential to continuously plan for increased capacity. This could involve adding more servers, expanding storage, or optimizing content delivery networks to ensure that the platform can scale efficiently.

Security Upgrades Regularly evaluate and implement **security patches** to safeguard your platform from vulnerabilities, especially as new threats emerge in the cybersecurity landscape.

By following these best practices, your video streaming platform will remain resilient, secure, and capable of adapting to future demands and technological advancements.

Deploying and maintaining a video streaming platform requires careful consideration of hosting options, CI/CD pipelines, monitoring, and future-proofing strategies. Whether you choose cloud hosting or on-premise solutions, setting up automated deployment processes and robust monitoring systems ensures that the platform operates smoothly and remains scalable.

By following industry best practices, you can not only keep your platform running efficiently but also ensure that it evolves with user demands and technology trends, leading to long-term success in the competitive video streaming market.

Chapter 13

Monetization Strategies

Monetizing a video streaming platform is one of the most critical elements for ensuring its long-term sustainability and success. There are several monetization strategies available, each suited to different types of content, user bases, and business goals. The choice of monetization model can significantly impact user experience, platform growth, and revenue generation. This chapter explores the two most popular monetization models for video streaming platforms the **subscription-based model** and the **ad-supported model**. In addition, it will cover **integrating payment gateways**, **using AI for targeted ads**, and **case studies** of successful monetization practices from leading platforms.

Subscription-Based Model vs. Ad-Supported Streaming

The choice between a subscription-based model and an ad-supported model is one of the most fundamental decisions that will shape the overall business strategy of a video streaming platform. Both models come with their advantages and challenges, and understanding these differences is essential for making an informed decision.

Subscription-Based Model

The subscription-based model is one of the most widely used monetization strategies for video streaming platforms, especially for premium content or niche services. Under this model, users pay a recurring fee, usually on a monthly or yearly basis, in exchange for access to exclusive content or an ad-free experience.

There are several variations of the subscription-based model, such as

Flat-rate Subscription Users pay a fixed amount for unlimited access to all available content. This model is typically used by platforms like **Netflix** and **Spotify**, which offer a wide range of content for a fixed fee.

Tiered Subscription This approach allows users to choose from different pricing tiers based on the features or content they wish to access. For example, a **basic tier** might provide access to standard-definition videos, while a **premium tier** offers high-definition content and additional features such as offline viewing. Examples of services using this model include **Hulu** and **Amazon Prime Video**.

Freemium Model Some platforms offer a free tier with limited content or features and provide users the option to upgrade to a paid plan for full access. This model is used by platforms like **YouTube Premium** and **Twitch**.

The subscription-based model offers a predictable and consistent revenue stream, making it attractive for investors and content creators alike. However, it also requires platforms to continuously provide high-quality, engaging content to retain subscribers. A major challenge for subscription-based platforms is **user churn**, which occurs when subscribers cancel their memberships.

Ad-Supported Streaming

The ad-supported model, also known as **advertising-based video on demand (AVOD)**, allows users to access content for free, but in exchange, they are shown advertisements during the video. This model is widely used by free streaming platforms such as **YouTube**, **Pluto TV**, and **Crackle**.

There are several forms of advertisements that can be integrated into an ad-supported streaming platform

Pre-roll Ads Advertisements that play before the video begins. These are typically 15-30 second ads.

Mid-roll Ads Advertisements that appear at intervals during the video. This type of ad is more common in long-form content, such as movies or TV shows.

Post-roll Ads Advertisements shown at the end of a video. These ads are often shorter and provide an opportunity for advertisers to reach users who have already engaged with the content.

Display Ads Banner or pop-up ads that appear on the screen during the video. These are less intrusive than pre-roll or mid-roll ads but can still be effective in generating revenue.

The ad-supported model can provide a steady income stream, especially if the platform attracts a large and engaged user base. One of the key benefits of this model is that users can access content for free, which may lead to higher user acquisition. However, the success of an ad-supported platform relies heavily on the ability to attract advertisers and effectively target them to the right audience.

Integrating Payment Gateways

Regardless of the monetization model, seamless payment integration is crucial for collecting subscription fees or handling transactions for premium content. Choosing the right **payment gateway** will ensure smooth, secure, and frictionless transactions for users while maximizing revenue for the platform.

Stripe and PayPal

Stripe and **PayPal** are two of the most commonly used payment gateways for video streaming platforms. Both services offer robust APIs that make it easy to integrate payment processing into your platform.

Stripe Known for its ease of use and scalability, Stripe allows video streaming platforms to accept a wide variety of payment methods, including credit and debit cards, bank transfers, and even digital wallets like Apple Pay and Google Pay. Stripe also offers tools for subscription management, fraud detection, and recurring billing, making it ideal for platforms that operate on a subscription model.

PayPal PayPal is another popular choice for handling payments. It is widely recognized and trusted by users around the world. Like Stripe, PayPal supports subscription payments, recurring billing, and one-time payments. One advantage of PayPal is its global reach, as it is available in over 200 markets worldwide. However, PayPal can have slightly higher transaction fees than Stripe, making it less ideal for certain platforms.

Cryptocurrency Payments

In addition to traditional payment methods, some video streaming platforms are beginning to accept

cryptocurrency as a payment option. With the rise of digital currencies such as **Bitcoin** and **Ethereum**, accepting cryptocurrency can open up new avenues for attracting a tech-savvy audience and provide an additional layer of privacy and security for users.

Cryptocurrency payments can be integrated through third-party payment processors like **BitPay** or **CoinGate**, which handle the complexity of cryptocurrency transactions and convert them into local currencies if necessary.

Using AI for Targeted Ads

Artificial Intelligence (AI) plays a pivotal role in optimizing monetization strategies for video streaming platforms. Through **AI-based targeted advertising** and **personalized content recommendations**, platforms can increase engagement, maximize ad revenues, and improve the overall user experience.

AI-Based Targeted Ads

Targeted advertising allows streaming platforms to show users ads that are relevant to their interests, increasing the likelihood that the ads will be viewed and acted upon. AI algorithms can analyze user data, such as **watch history**, **search behavior**, and

demographic information, to segment audiences and serve personalized ads.

For example, a streaming platform could use AI to show users ads for fitness equipment if they frequently watch workout videos, or ads for travel destinations if they often watch travel documentaries. This precision makes ad inventory more valuable to advertisers and increases the potential for higher CPM (cost per thousand impressions) rates.

Personalized Content Recommendations

Personalized content recommendations powered by AI improve user engagement by suggesting videos or series based on a user's past viewing habits. Machine learning algorithms analyze **user preferences**, **watch history**, and **similar viewers** to suggest new content that is likely to interest the user.

Platforms like **Netflix** and **YouTube** are masters at this, using AI to generate recommendation engines that not only keep users engaged but also increase the time spent on the platform. The more content a user watches, the more data the AI has to improve its recommendations, creating a positive feedback loop.

Case Studies of Successful Streaming

To better understand how different monetization strategies work in practice, let's look at a few real-world examples of successful video streaming platforms and their monetization approaches

Netflix – Subscription Model

Netflix is the prime example of a **subscription-based monetization model**. The platform uses a tiered pricing model, offering different subscription plans based on the number of devices a user can stream from and the video quality (e.g., standard definition vs. ultra-high definition). By offering a free trial period and providing high-quality original content, Netflix has been able to achieve massive global growth. It is one of the most successful subscription-based streaming platforms, with over 200 million subscribers worldwide.

YouTube – Ad-Supported Model

YouTube operates under an **ad-supported model**, where users can watch videos for free but are shown ads in between or before content. YouTube's ad revenue is generated through **Google Ads**, which allows advertisers to target specific demographics. The platform also offers YouTube Premium, a subscription-based model that provides an ad-free experience.

YouTube has successfully monetized its platform through a combination of both ad revenue and premium subscriptions.

Twitch – Hybrid Model

Twitch, primarily a live-streaming platform for gamers, uses a hybrid monetization model that combines **subscriptions**, **ads**, and **donations**. Viewers can subscribe to their favorite streamers for a monthly fee, with streamers earning a percentage of the subscription revenue. Twitch also generates income from advertisements shown during live streams, as well as donations from users who wish to support streamers directly.

Choosing the right monetization strategy for a video streaming platform is a critical decision that will affect the platform's growth, user experience, and long-term sustainability. Whether you opt for a **subscription-based model**, an **ad-supported model**, or a hybrid approach, it is essential to consider factors like user engagement, content quality, and audience targeting. Using **payment gateway integrations**, utilizing **AI** for personalized recommendations and targeted ads, and learning from **successful case studies** can help ensure that your monetization efforts are both effective and sustainable. Ultimately, the goal is to create a balance that provides value to users while driving profitability for the platform.

Chapter 14

Future of Video Streaming

The video streaming industry has evolved dramatically over the past two decades. What started as a way to watch TV shows and movies on-demand has transformed into a global entertainment powerhouse, encompassing a wide variety of content types such as live events, user-generated videos, and even virtual reality (VR) and augmented reality (AR) experiences. As we move into the future, several emerging technologies are poised to shape the next generation of video streaming, offering new opportunities for content creators, distributors, and viewers alike. This chapter will explore some of the most important advancements, including **5G**, **AI**, **VR/AR streaming**, and **blockchain**. Additionally, we will discuss the future of **user engagement**, **content consumption trends**, and **opportunities for innovation** within the video streaming industry.

Emerging Technologies Shaping the Future

5G and Its Impact on Streaming

5G is the fifth generation of mobile network technology, offering significantly faster download and upload speeds compared to its predecessor, 4G. It is expected to be a game-changer for video streaming, particularly for mobile users, as it enables smoother, higher-quality streaming experiences even in areas with previously unreliable connections.

One of the most exciting aspects of 5G is its **low latency**, which refers to the minimal delay in data transmission between devices. This is especially important for live streaming, where a few seconds of delay can negatively impact user experience. With 5G, viewers can enjoy near-instantaneous streaming of live events, such as sports or concerts, without the annoying buffering or lag that often occurs on slower networks.

Furthermore, 5G's ability to handle large amounts of data simultaneously will make it easier to stream content in **higher resolutions**, such as **4K** and **8K**, on mobile devices without sacrificing quality. The improved bandwidth also enables **multi-streaming** experiences, where users can watch multiple video feeds simultaneously, which could be particularly useful for sports broadcasts or interactive video content.

As the global rollout of 5G continues, it will open up new possibilities for **mobile-first content**, where platforms can optimize their services for the unique needs of on-the-go viewers. This shift could drive the rise of **location-based content**, where users access streams tailored to their geographical location, providing more personalized and relevant experiences.

AI and Machine Learning in Video Streaming

Artificial Intelligence (AI) and machine learning are already playing a significant role in video streaming, and their influence is expected to grow exponentially in the coming years. These technologies are used for a wide range of purposes, from content recommendations to content moderation, video compression, and customer support.

One of the most notable applications of AI in video streaming is **content recommendation algorithms**. Platforms like **Netflix**, **YouTube**, and **Spotify** use machine learning to analyze user behavior and suggest content based on their interests, watching habits, and interactions. By continually refining these algorithms, platforms can increase user engagement, reduce churn rates, and personalize the viewing experience to a greater degree.

AI is also used for **video compression**. Video files can be enormous, especially for high-definition content, and transmitting these files over the internet can be a significant challenge. AI-driven video compression techniques, such as those being developed in conjunction with the **H.265 (HEVC)** and **AV1** codecs, are making it possible to stream high-quality videos with less data usage and fewer buffering issues. These technologies are crucial as the demand for higher resolution and more immersive content increases.

Furthermore, AI is transforming **content moderation**. With the rise of user-generated content, platforms face challenges in monitoring and filtering inappropriate or harmful videos. AI algorithms are being trained to detect objectionable content, including hate speech, violence, and explicit material, to ensure a safer viewing environment for users. This will be an essential part of maintaining platform integrity as user engagement continues to increase.

VR/AR Streaming The Next Frontier

Virtual Reality (VR) and Augmented Reality (AR) are emerging as major disruptors in the video streaming space. While both technologies have primarily been associated with gaming and entertainment, they are now being explored for more interactive and immersive video experiences.

Virtual Reality (VR) involves creating a completely immersive digital environment where users can interact with virtual worlds through a VR headset. In video streaming, VR can be used to offer **360-degree video** experiences, where users can explore environments, events, or stories from all angles. This can be especially appealing for **live events**, such as concerts or sports games, where users can feel like they are physically present in the venue, experiencing the action in real-time.

Augmented Reality (AR), on the other hand, overlays digital content on the real world. In the context of video streaming, AR can be used to improve storytelling by adding interactive elements to the content. For instance, during a movie or sports event, AR can project live statistics, interactive characters, or additional scenes that viewers can interact with using their smartphones or AR glasses.

Both VR and AR require specialized equipment, such as headsets or AR glasses, and the technology is still in its early stages. However, as the hardware becomes more affordable and accessible, and the content quality improves, VR and AR streaming could revolutionize the way we experience entertainment.

Blockchain and Decentralized Platforms

Blockchain technology, which underpins cryptocurrencies like **Bitcoin** and **Ethereum**, has the potential to transform the video streaming industry in profound ways. Blockchain offers **decentralized**, **transparent**, and **secure** systems that can remove intermediaries, reduce costs, and give content creators more control over their intellectual property.

In traditional video streaming, content creators, distributors, and viewers rely on central platforms (e.g., **YouTube**, **Netflix**) to access content, which often involves high fees and a lack of direct communication between creators and audiences. Blockchain enables a **decentralized streaming model** where content is directly shared between creators and viewers, and payments are handled through smart contracts or cryptocurrencies. This system can eliminate the need for middlemen and ensure that creators receive fair compensation for their work, as every transaction is recorded on an immutable ledger.

Moreover, blockchain can be used to combat **piracy** by providing a secure and verifiable way to track content ownership and distribution. This can help prevent unauthorized distribution and ensure that content creators maintain control over their work.

While the implementation of blockchain in video streaming is still in its infancy, there are a few pioneering platforms, such as **Theta** and **Livepeer**, that are already exploring this approach, offering decentralized video delivery networks and rewarding users with cryptocurrency for sharing their bandwidth.

Trends in User Engagement

As the video streaming industry continues to grow, several key trends in **user engagement** and **content consumption** are emerging.

One of the most significant trends is the **shift toward shorter-form content**. With the rise of platforms like

TikTok and **Instagram Reels**, audiences are increasingly seeking bite-sized, easily digestible videos that can be consumed on the go. This shift is especially apparent among younger viewers, who prefer content that can be quickly watched, shared, and interacted with.

In contrast, long-form content, such as documentaries, feature films, and original series, continues to thrive on platforms like **Netflix** and **Amazon Prime Video**, which invest heavily in exclusive and high-quality content. However, as attention spans shorten, streaming platforms are experimenting with ways to make long-form content more interactive and engaging, such as by incorporating **choose-your-own-adventure** style narratives or integrating immersive VR/AR elements.

Another trend is the growing importance of **interactive streaming**. Services like **Twitch** and **YouTube Live** have popularized live streaming, allowing users to engage with content in real-time through chat, donations, and even participating in events. This interactive element is becoming increasingly important for fostering community and user loyalty, especially in the context of gaming, esports, and user-generated content.

Opportunities for Innovation

The future of video streaming is full of exciting opportunities for innovation. One of the key areas ripe for disruption is **content discovery**. As streaming platforms amass vast libraries of content, finding relevant videos can be a daunting task for users. AI-powered recommendation engines are already addressing this issue, but there is room for improvement. Future platforms might incorporate advanced **voice search**, **gesture control**, or even **emotion-sensing technology** to allow users to discover content more naturally and intuitively.

Another area for innovation is the **integration of live streaming** with **e-commerce**. Platforms like **Amazon** have already experimented with shoppable videos, where viewers can purchase products directly through the video content. This trend could become more prevalent, especially in niches like fashion, tech reviews, or cooking, where products are frequently featured in videos.

Furthermore, there are growing opportunities for platforms to experiment with **user-generated content monetization**. Platforms like **TikTok** have already shown how creators can earn money through ads, partnerships, and sponsorships. As user-generated content continues to dominate the digital landscape, platforms will need to explore new revenue-sharing models and tools that enable creators to earn a sustainable income.

The future of video streaming is brimming with possibilities. Emerging technologies such as **5G**, **AI**, **VR/AR**, and **blockchain** are set to revolutionize the way content is delivered, consumed, and monetized. As platforms experiment with new ways to engage users, drive innovation, and leverage data, the streaming industry will continue to evolve rapidly. While challenges remain, particularly in areas like content piracy and user privacy, the future looks bright for video streaming as it continues to grow and adapt to the needs of its diverse and ever-evolving audience.

THE END